The Kebab Cookbook: Savory, Health-Conscious and Simple Mediterranean Diet Recipes on a Stick

Disclaimer and Terms of Use: Effort has been made to ensure that the information in this book is accurate and complete, however, the author and the publisher do not warrant the accuracy of the information, text and graphics contained within the book due to the rapidly changing nature of science, research, known and unknown facts and Internet. The Author and the publisher do not hold any responsibility for errors, omissions or contrary interpretation of the subject matter herein. This book is presented solely for motivational and informational purposes only.

Table of Contents

Capers

Ingredients:
- 1 C fresh mozzarella balls
- ½ C cherry tomatoes
- ¼ C sun dried tomatoes
- ½ bunch basil leaves

Ingredients:

I.   These are really pretty simple. You will alternate each ingredient on soaked skewers and add to the grill for JUST 25-30 seconds on each side to singe

II.   Drizzle with olive oil just before serving

Corn Dogs

Ingredients:
- 1 ¼ C cornmeal
- ¾ C whole wheat pastry flour
- 1 ½ tsp. baking powder
- ½ tsp. salt
- 2 T honey
- 2 eggs
- ¾ C milk
- turkey or chicken hot dogs
- 2 qt. grape seed oil

Directions:

I.   Heat your oil in a skillet and skewer your hot dogs
II.   Add your cornmeal and other dry ingredients into a jar or bowl with a lid and shake well
III.   Now add in your wet ingredients and shake well again
IV.   Open lid and stir a few times
V.   Roll skewered hot dogs in a little bit of dry flour
VI.   Then dip into batter and fry until golden brown

Watermelon and Feta

Ingredients:
- seedless watermelon
- block of feta cheese
- 1 T olive oil
- 1 tsp. salt and pepper to taste
- basil leaves

Directions:

I.   Slice your watermelon into square pieces, and mix in a bowl with the olive oil and salt and pepper
II.   Cut the feta into 16-18 square pieces
III.   Add one feta then one watermelon square and repeat
IV.   Serve cool

Cilantro Beef

Ingredients:
- 1 lb. beef sirloin
- 1 pkg. flatbread wraps
- 1 diced tomato
- 2 C arugula

Marinade

- 1/3 C soy sauce
- 1/4 C fresh cilantro, chopped
- 4 tsp. fish sauce
- 1 1/2 tsp. brown sugar
- 1 tsp. canola oil
- 3 T minced garlic

Dipping sauce

- 1/2 C sour cream
- 1/4 C minced cilantro
- 1 T lime juice

Directions:

I. You can start by preparing your marinade, which is really pretty simple; you are going to add all of your ingredients into your blender or food processor and puree until pastey
II. Marinade your beef slices in the fridge for about 3-4 hours
III. Place your marinated beef on the skewers and grill until cooked
IV. Prepare your dipping sauce—add all of the ingredients in the list and stir well; when done, add to your fridge until ready to serve

Sausage and Peach Skewers

Ingredients:
- 1 lb. chicken sausage
- sun dried tomatoes
- mozzarella balls
- ripe peaches, pitted and sliced

Directions:

I.   Pierce sausages with the skewers, and cook on low heat, on all sides over heat on skillet
II. Grill the pitted peach sliced for a few seconds on each side
III. Remove sausage from skewers and slice
IV. And add one peach slice, the sausage bite, alternating until done

Avocado Creamed Tuna

Ingredients:

- sliced fresh tuna
- ripe avocado
- lime
- chili
- mint leaves
- basil
- dried oregano
- salt and pepper to taste

Directions:

I.   Start by slicing your tuna into bite size squares, and do the same thing with your avocado
II.   Place the two ingredients in separate bowls and marinate with juice, oil and pepper and the rest of ingredients
III. Start your grill while these are marinating
IV.   Skewer the foods, one after the other, tuna, avocado, lime repeat
V.   Grill until seared and cook on each side
VI.   Serve

Grilled Flowers

Ingredients:
- 1 head broccoli
- ½ head cauliflower
- 1 red onion, wedged
- 1 tomato, wedged
- 3 T chickpeas
- ½ C yogurt
- 3 T chickpeas
- 2 T lemon juice
- 2 T canola oil
- 1 T garlic paste
- 1 T ginger paste
- 1 tsp. masala
- 1 tsp. paprika
- ½ tsp. turmeric
- 1 tsp. coriander powder
- salt and pepper to taste

Directions:

I. Cut your broccoli and cauliflower, making about 2 C of each
II. Boil your vegetables (add salt to taste) for no more than 30 seconds and drain
III. Whisk your marinade ingredients and coat over vegetables
IV. Let sit marinating in fridge for about 30 minutes and add in other vegetables and set for another 10-15 minutes
V. Skewer your vegetables
VI. Grill, searing both sides

Grilled Eggplant

Ingredients:
- eggplant
- breadcrumbs
- grated parmesan cheese
- EVOO
- salt to taste

Directions:

I. Slice your eggplant
II. Let open eggplant slices sit for about 20-25 minutes
III. Mix the other ingredients, and add to the top of the eggplant
IV. Roll slices onto skewers, and grill

Green and Orange Kabobs

Ingredients:
- 2 T honey
- ½ orange, wedged
- ¼ C orange juice
- fresh ginger, grated
- ½ cucumber, sliced
- 1 lb. scallops
- salt and pepper to taste

Directions:

I. Set your grill to hot, and prepare the honey and orange juice
II. Thread your scallops and orange wedges on skewers and brush honey and juice on skewered scallops
III. Grill for 4-5 minutes on each side

Sub on a Stick

Ingredients:

- whole wheat bread (rounded)
- cubed cheddar
- roma tomatoes
- lettuce
- lunch meat of your choice

Directions:

I.   Take small bite size amounts of each ingredients
II. Skewer each ingredient in the order of bread, cheese, meat, lettuce, bread

Side Salad on a Stick

Ingredients:
- carrots, sliced
- 1 cucumber, sliced
- ½ head lettuce, sliced or cubed
- 1 C grape or cherry tomatoes

Directions:

Take one of each of the ingredients and add to skewer one at a time and repeat

Greek Skewers

Ingredients:
- 1 ½ lbs. boneless chicken breast, stripped
- 4 T EVOO
- 4 T minced garlic
- 1 tsp. dried oregano
- 1 tsp. salt and pepper to taste
- 2 T lemon juice
- ½ red onion, quartered
- 1 bell pepper sliced

Directions:

I. Marinate your chicken in the liquids and set aside
II. Heat your grill and skewer your chicken, onions and peppers
III. Grill on each side for about 8-10 minutes or until chicken is cooked

Mustard Sprouts

Ingredients:
- 1 lb. sprouts
- 2 T mustard
- 2 T olive oil
- salt and pepper to taste

Directions:

I.   Boil your sprouts for 3-5 minutes and drain
II.   Trim sprouts and coat in mustard
III.   Add to skewers and grill on all sides

Cilantro Pesto

Ingredients:
- 2 bunches pesto
- 2 C baby spinach
- 1 lemon
- juice from lemon
- 2 T pine nuts
- ¼ C parmesan cheese
- 1 ½ C olive oil
- salt and pepper to taste

Directions:

I.   Add everything but the olive oil into your food processor or blender, start to blend or stir and add in oil a little bit at a time

II.   Season with salt and pepper

III. Brush pesto over the spring on skewers

IV.   Grill on both sides

Chicken Kabob

Ingredients:
- 2 chicken breasts, bite size
- ½ C Caesar dressing
- 2 slices whole wheat bread
- 2 T EVOO
- 1 tsp. garlic salt
- romaine hearts
- ¼ C parmesan cheese
- salt and pepper to taste

Directions:

I.   Add chicken and ¼ C of the dressing into a Ziploc bag and shake. Let marinate in fridge for about 45 minutes to an hour

II. Toast the bread, and sprinkle salt, pepper and garlic onto bread and toast it

III. Prepare your grill, and skewer the chicken

IV. Add lettuce on top of toasted bread and chicken and serve over bread

Berries on a Stick

Ingredients:
- basil
- prosciutto, chunked
- papaya, chunked
- raspberry

Directions:

I.   Brush basil over everything and add everything to small toothpicks or skewers
II. Serve

Grilled Sweet Potatoes

Ingredients:

- sweet potatoes
- 1 T coconut oil
- coconut flakes
- greek yogurt

Directions:

I.   Heat your grill
II.   Boil the potatoes in a pot of water for about 8-10 minutes, drain and skewer
III.   Grill for about 4-5 minutes

Dog on a Stick and Dip

Ingredients:
- 1 pkg. hot dogs
- 1 avocado, diced
- lime juice
- square size tortilla chips
- ½ C sour cream
- 1 avocado
- ½ C cilantro
- 1 T capers
- salt and pepper to taste

Directions:

I.   Skewer your first set of ingredients, and create the dip using the remaining ingredients

II.   Grill skewers and use dip to garnish

Thai Shrimp

Ingredients:
- 1 jalapeño, stemmed
- 1 T minced garlic
- 1 C coconut milk
- 1/3 C fresh mint
- 1 T fish sauce
- jumbo shrimp, deveined
- 1 avocado, peeled and pitted

Directions:

I.   Make your marinade by adding everything but the shrimp to the food processor or blender and blend for about 2 minutes,

II.   Pour marinade over the shrimp in a bowl and set in fridge for about 1-2 hours

III. Start your grill and start adding the marinating shrimp to skewers and grill

IV.   Grill on both sides for 6-8 minutes

V.   Serve

Berries and Dip

Ingredients:
- 1 pint strawberries
- 1 pint blueberries

Directions:

I.   Alternate between berries and strawberries on skewers and refrigerate

II.   Use greek yogurt for dipping sauce

Berry Balls

Ingredients:
- red grapes
- green grapes
- greek yogurt

Directions:

Alternate the different grapes on skewers and dip with the greek yogurt

Pumpkin Pie Sticks

Ingredients:
- 4 unpacked pie shells
- 1 egg
- ¾ brown sugar
- ½ tsp. salt
- 1 tsp. vanilla extract
- 2 ½ tsp. spice powder
- 2 eggs
- 1 can pumpkin
- 1 can condensed milk

Directions:
I.   Preheat your oven to 375 degrees
II.   Roll out the pie crusts and make small circles or cutouts
III.   Add your pumpkin to the center and add sticks
IV.   Add top layer of pie crust and press ends together, brush whisked egg over tops
V.   Bake on baking sheet for 8-12 minutes

Banana Sticks

Ingredients:
- banana
- chocolate chips
- granola

Directions:

I.   Melt the chocolate
II.   Freeze bananas on a stick
III.   Roll bananas on a stick in chocolate, then in granola oats
IV.   Freeze for another 10-12 minutes
V.   Serve cold

presso Pops

Ingredients:
- 1 ½ C coffee (cold or room temperature)
- 1 ½ C milk
- 1 T syrup

Directions:

I.   Mix everything in a bowl, then pour into a mold
II.   Freeze with sticks on the ends

10697087R00018

Made in the USA
San Bernardino, CA
30 November 2018